Founded in 1865, Ave Maria Press is a ministry of the United States Province of Holy Cross.

www.avemariapress.com

Paperback: ISBN-13 978-1-59471-584-6

Cover and text design by K. H. Bonelli.

Printed and bound in the United States of America.

FOREWORD

As a longtime fan of Daniel Mitsui's work and a confessed adult-coloring-book geek, I was thrilled when Mitsui made a few coloring sheets available on his website. In an interview with *Aleteia* he explained that he had included the sheets, "not because of this [adult coloring] craze but because of the dearth of dignified coloring material available from religious publishers and homeschooling resources."

I quickly downloaded the available sheets and spent many contented hours with them and some high-quality, color-saturated pencils. While I could in no way duplicate the intensity of Mitsui's own vivid work, I nevertheless found that spending time within his images brought me first into a place of deep focus, then into relaxation, and finally into the stillness that comes with prayerful adoration. It is very easy to fall into prayer while working on these images, and working with these images gives one a small taste of what icon writers describe of their contemplative work.

Mitsui has said that he doesn't think there should be a difference between coloring books for adults and for children, adding, "I think everyone, no matter what age, should have good artwork." That generous philosophy makes me all the more admiring of Daniel Mitsui and his work and all the happier to imagine the intergenerational family projects that might flow from this collection. I wish each purchaser many blissful hours inside these heavenly lines.

Elizabeth Scalia

April 2016, Montauk, New York

US Editor-in-Chief of *Aleteia* and

author of *Strange Gods: Unmasking the Idols of Everyday Life*

INTRODUCTION

Catholic tradition maintains that the Rosary of the Blessed Virgin Mary was given to St. Dominic by the Blessed Virgin in the thirteenth century. The devotion became especially popular in the late fifteenth century, following the preaching and writing of the Dominican Alanus de la Roche. The first Rosary Confraternities were founded, and the first devotional books dedicated to the Holy Rosary were circulated. These included both illuminated manuscripts and books made on the newly-invented printing press.

By that time, the Holy Rosary had attained its familiar modern form: 150 recitations of the Ave Maria divided into fifteen decades, each preceded by a recitation of the Pater Noster. Usually each decade was associated with an event in the life of Jesus or Mary. The selection of events varied somewhat; for example, some of the faithful prayed the Last Judgment as the final mystery, while others prayed the Coronation of the Blessed Virgin. Certain works of art from the late fifteenth century illustrate events that correspond exactly to the now-familiar Joyful, Sorrowful, and Glorious Mysteries.

This coloring book is formatted to resemble one of the early devotional books dedicated to the Holy Rosary. A German volume printed in 1483, which surrounds each illustrated Mystery with a border of ten roses, was an especially strong influence on its design.

The illustrated Mysteries are taken from a series of three large (9"× 12") drawings that I made in 2011. The original works I drew in ink of calfskin vellum; these are now held in a private collection. Many of the decorative borders and ancillary pictures are taken from other drawings, rearranged into the compositions here in the manner of printers' blocks. All of the artwork originally came from my own hand.

THE JOYFUL MYSTERIES

Each of the three large drawings that I made in 2011 to illustrate the Mysteries of the Holy Rosary is composed of a title, five quatrefoils, and four roundels inside a decorative framework.

For the Joyful Mysteries, the framework takes the form of an enclosed garden, one of the mystical titles of the Blessed Virgin. It is filled with tiny plants and animals, resembling those in fifteenth-century Flemish millefleur tapestries.

A small scene of a unicorn hunt as an allegory of the Incarnation is included in the *bas-de-page*, or "bottom of the page." This allegory is explained in the text of the bestiary, a medieval encyclopedia of animal symbolism. It was believed that a unicorn could only be caught by a virgin alone in the forest; the beast, which evades the mightiest hunters, embraces the virgin and goes to sleep in her lap. This is a symbol of Jesus Christ, who descended to the womb of the Blessed Virgin Mary.

The five quatrefoils contain scenes of the Annunciation, the Visitation, the Nativity of Christ, the Presentation in the Temple, and Christ among the Elders. Artists whose work informed their composition include the Boucicaut Master, the Limbourg Brothers, Absolon Stumme, Johann Koerbecke, and Jacquelin de Montluçon.

The four major prophets—Isaiah, Jeremiah, Ezekiel, and Daniel—appear in roundels between the larger scenes.

ANNUNCIATION
TO THE BLESSED
VIRGIN MARY

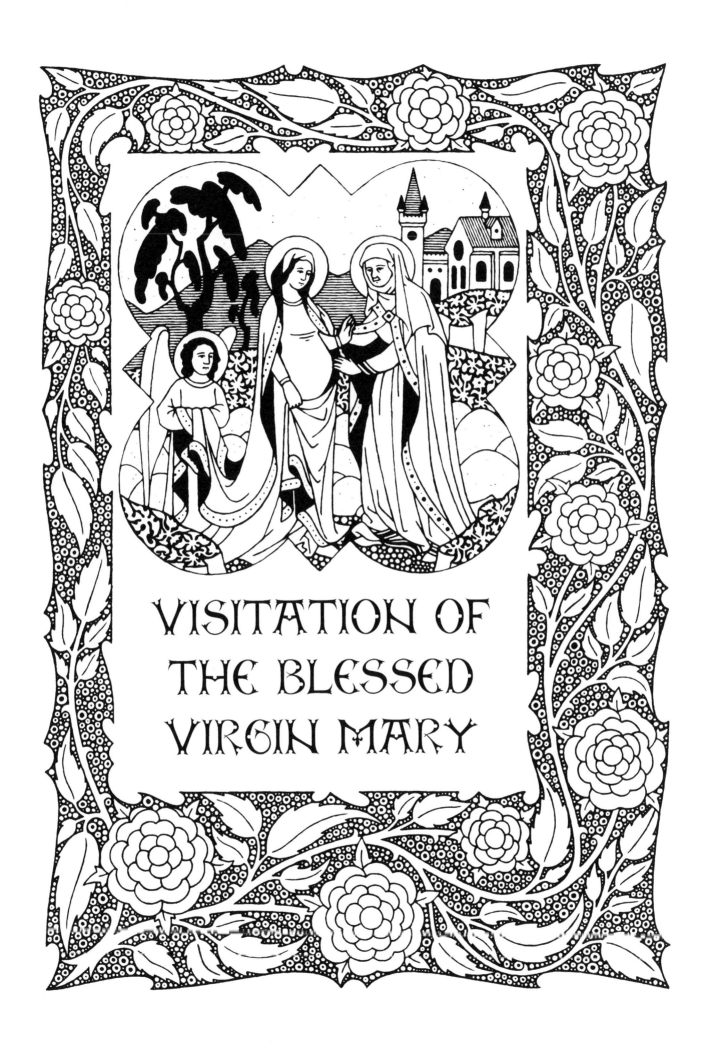

VISITATION OF
THE BLESSED
VIRGIN MARY

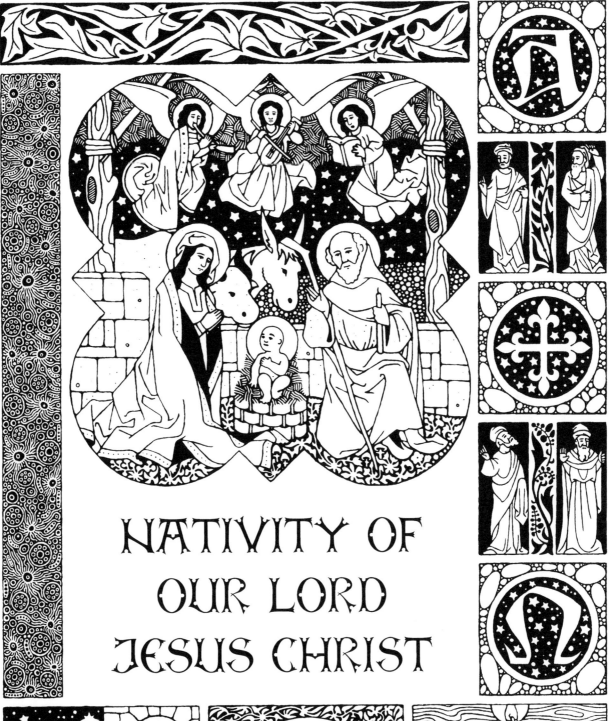

NATIVITY OF OUR LORD JESUS CHRIST

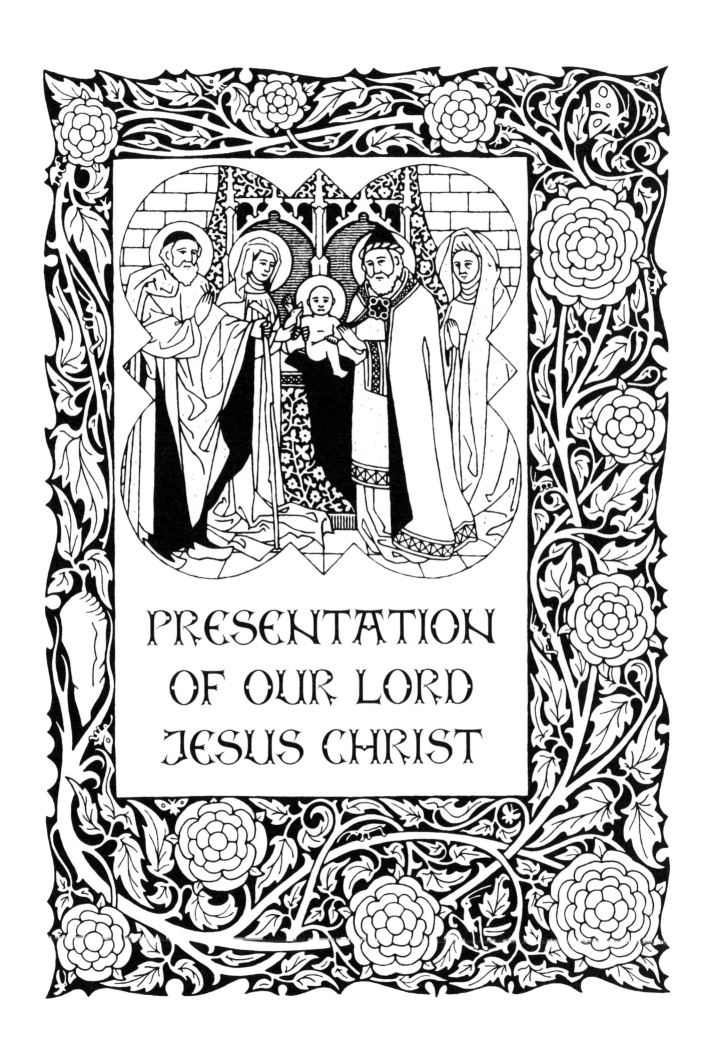

PRESENTATION
OF OUR LORD
JESUS CHRIST

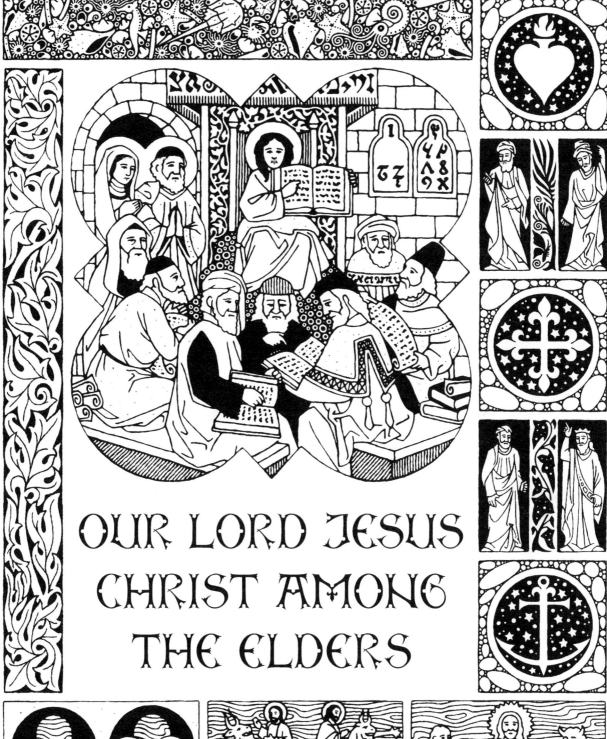

OUR LORD JESUS
CHRIST AMONG
THE ELDERS

THE SORROWFUL MYSTERIES

My drawing of the Sorrowful Mysteries of the Rosary was influenced by paintings by Hans Holbein the Elder, Jan Polack, Hieronymus Bosch, Gerard David, Martin Schongauer, Rogier van der Weyden, the Master of the Peterborough Psalter, the Master of St. Severin, and Nikolaus Obilman.

The four winged creatures in the roundels are symbols of the four evangelists. The man represents St. Matthew, whose book begins with a genealogy, a record of men. The ox is a sacrificial animal, and the Gospel of St. Luke opens with St. Zachary offering sacrifice at the Temple. The lion represents St. Mark, whose book begins with a voice crying, or roaring like a lion, in the wilderness. The eagle was believed to gaze directly into the sun, and the Gospel of St. John opens with insight into impossibly dazzling truths.

In the framework surrounding the Sorrowful Mysteries, I drew plants mentioned in the gospel accounts of the Passion of Our Lord Jesus Christ: olive (for the Garden of Gethsemane); hyssop; myrrh; grape (the source of wine and vinegar); the jujube tree, whose branches formed the Crown of Thorns; and a passionflower, which is so named because its various parts resemble the instruments of the Passion.

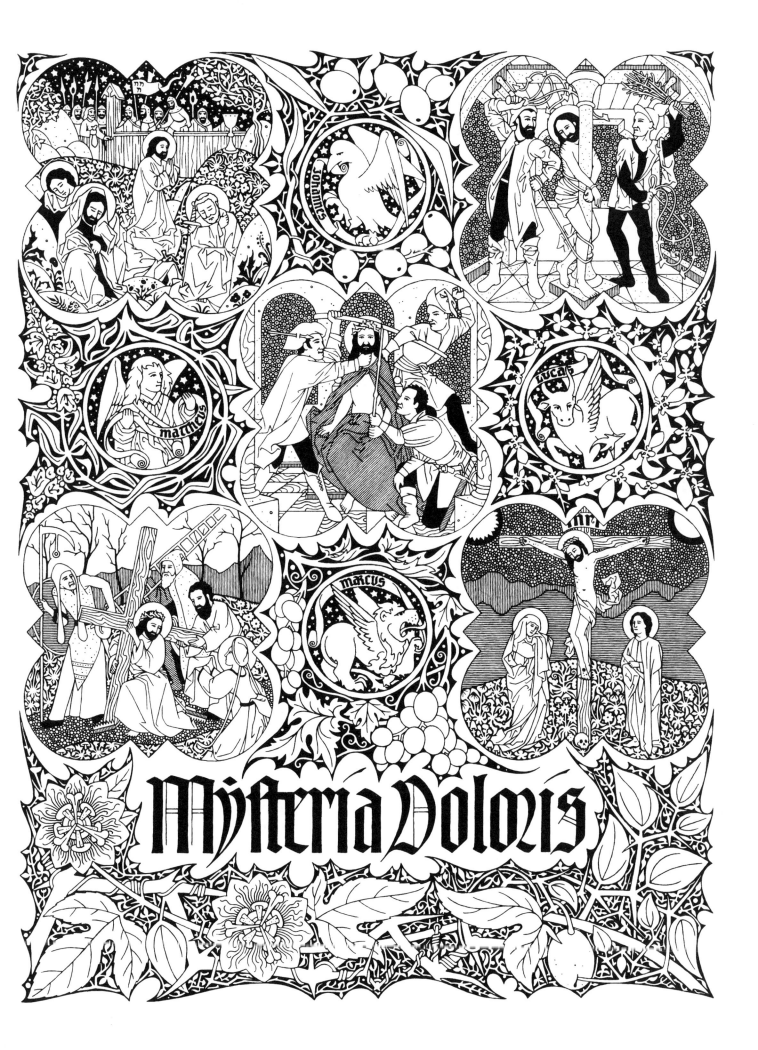

Mysteria Doloris

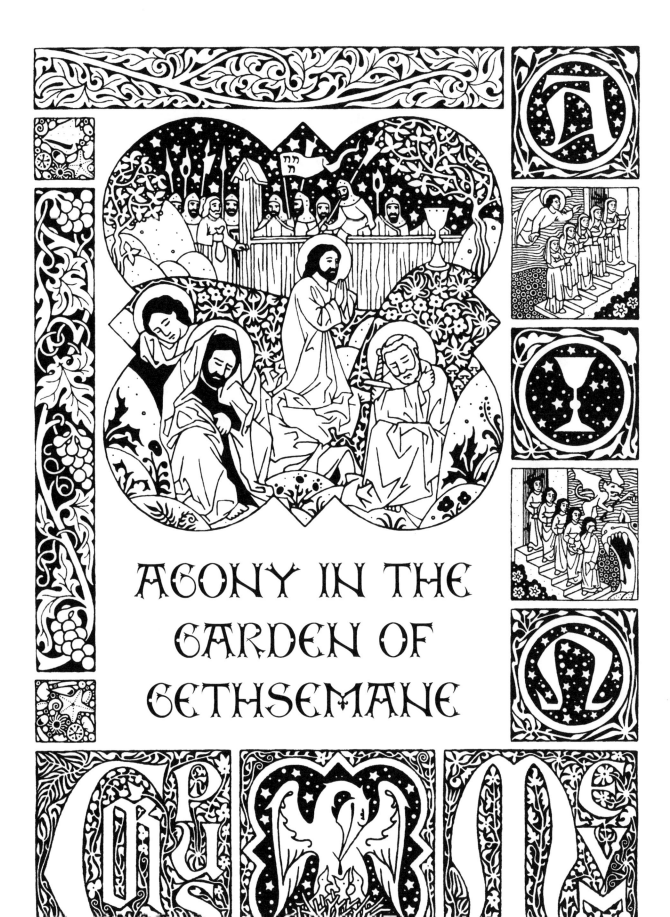

AGONY IN THE GARDEN OF GETHSEMANE

FLAGELLATION
OF OUR LORD
JESUS CHRIST

OUR LORD JESUS CHRIST CROWNED WITH THORNS

OUR LORD JESUS CHRIST CARRIES HIS CROSS

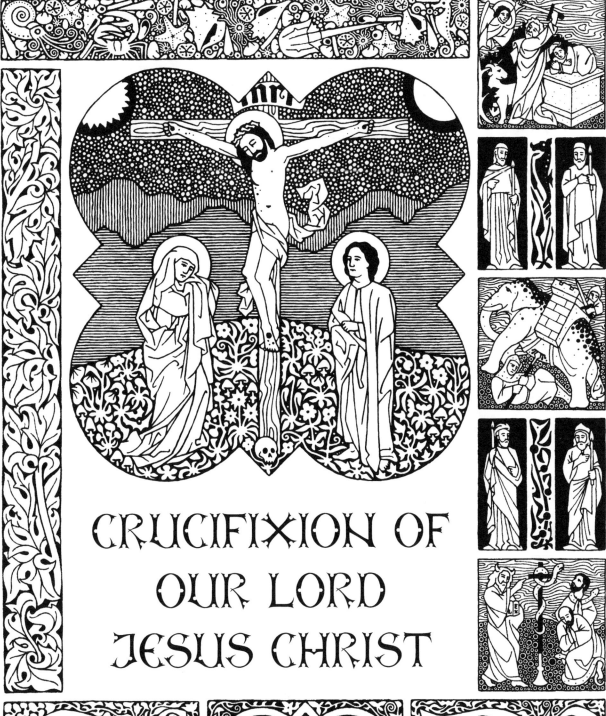

CRUCIFIXION OF OUR LORD JESUS CHRIST

The Glorious Mysteries

In my drawing of the Glorious Mysteries of the Rosary, the decorative framework is composed of vines, leaves, and tendrils. A butterfly in the *bas-de-page* symbolizes the Resurrection. The four great fathers of the Latin Church—St. Gregory the Great, St. Jerome, St. Augustine, and St. Ambrose—appear in roundels between the larger scenes.

St. Gregory wears a papal tiara. A dove perched on his shoulder represents the special help he received from the Holy Spirit in his work as a theologian and liturgist. St. Jerome, because he was ordained a priest of the diocese of Rome, wears the garb of a cardinal. He holds a model church in one hand, and an open book in the other; this is the Bible that he translated into Latin. St. Augustine holds a flaming heart pierced with two arrows, a reference to a passage in his Confessions: "Thou hadst pierced our hearts with Thy charity." St. Ambrose holds a scourge and is surrounded by bees, to indicate that he was a scourge of heretics and a mellifluous orator.

Artists whose work influenced this drawing include Dieric Bouts, Hans Multscher, the Master of the Life of the Virgin, the Master of the St. Lucy Legend, and the Master of the Salem Holy Altars.

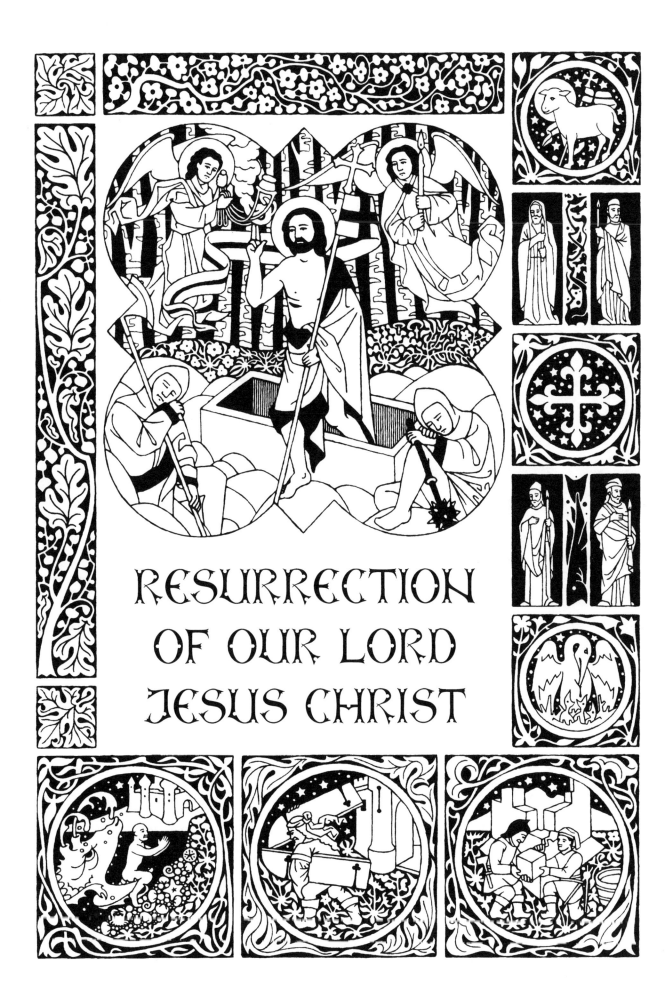

RESURRECTION
OF OUR LORD
JESUS CHRIST

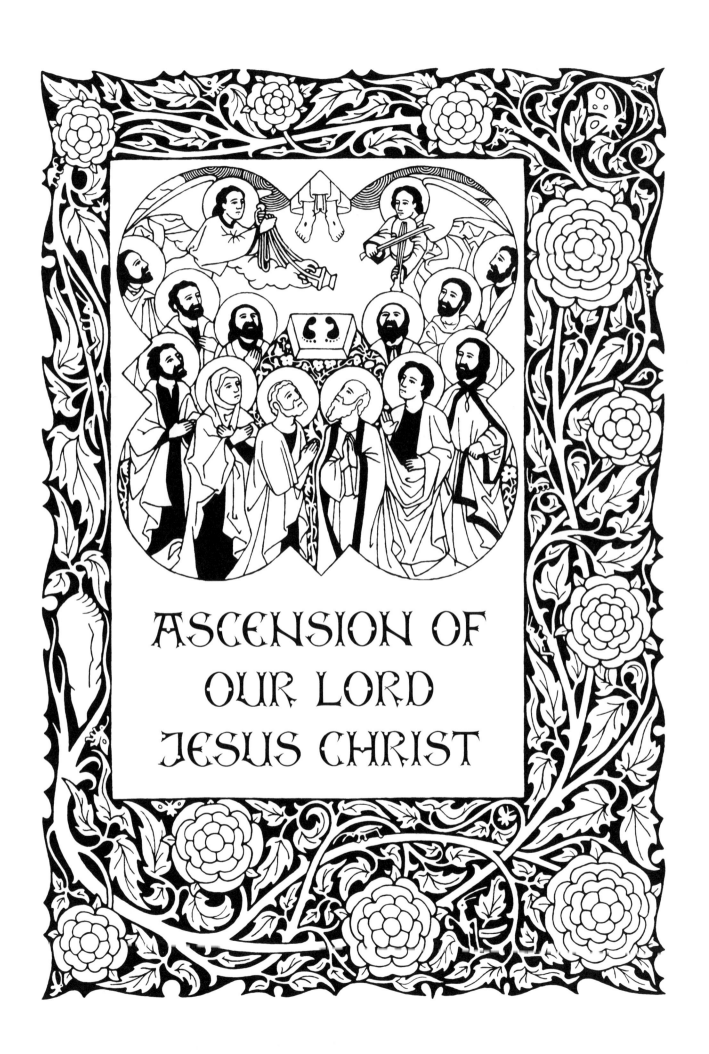

ASCENSION OF
OUR LORD
JESUS CHRIST

DESCENT OF THE
HOLY GHOST
AT PENTECOST

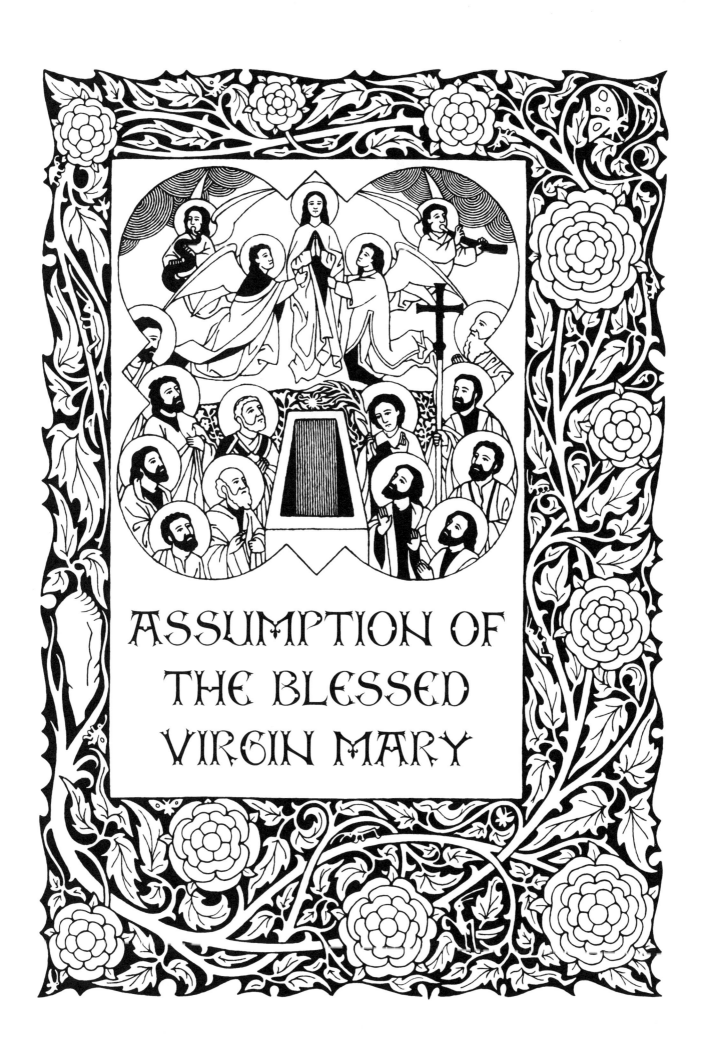

ASSUMPTION OF
THE BLESSED
VIRGIN MARY

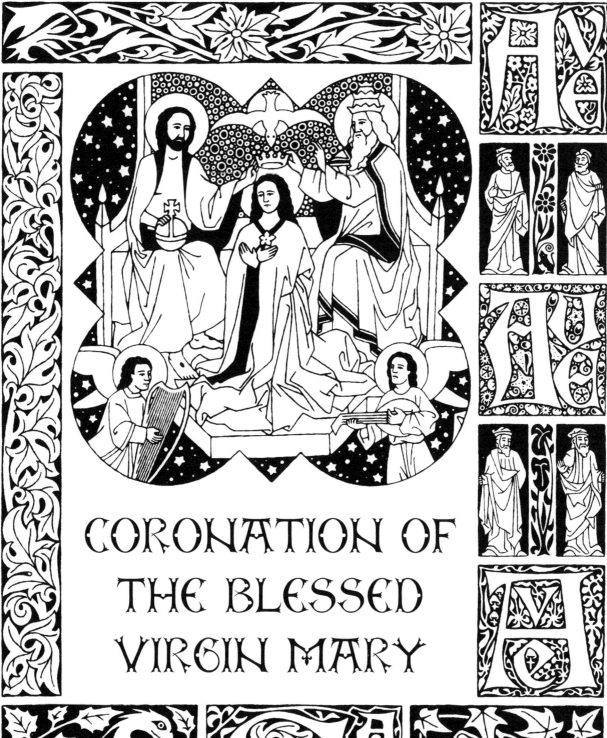

CORONATION OF THE BLESSED VIRGIN MARY

Artist Daniel Mitsui specializes in ink drawing. His meticulously detailed creations—created entirely by hand on paper or vellum—are held in collections worldwide. Since his baptism into the Catholic Church in 2004, he has focused most of his art on religious subjects.

Mitsui is a 2004 graduate of Dartmouth College (*cum laude* and senior fellow), where he studied drawing, oil painting, etching, lithography, wood carving, bookbinding, and film animation.

The Vatican commissioned Mitsui to illustrate a new edition of the Roman Pontifical in 2011. In 2012, he established Millefleur Press, an imprint for publishing fine books and broadsides of his artwork and typography. He is a prolific designer of custom bookplates.

Born in Georgia and raised in Illinois, Mitsui lives in Chicago with his wife, Michelle, and their three children.